The Journey of My Life

Ruins of Memories

Badradeen Mohammed

Contents

Dedication

This collection is dedicated to the ESOL department at City of Glasgow College for all their support throughout my writing journey, all its teachers and staff and especially the ones who taught me.

Special thanks also to the Seeds of Thought poetry family and my friend Tawona Sithole for their support and for allowing me to share my thoughts in their event at the CCA since 2012.

Special thanks also to all my language teachers throughout my journey of education. Special one to my English teacher at Altcbian Secondary School, Dr. Jaafer Abdul-Kareem, for planting the seeds of English creativity in my brain, to Colin McGuire for going over the pieces, and to everyone I've met throughout the journey of my life.

About the Author

Badradeen was born to a big family in the middle west of Sudan.

He spent his early childhood travelling between his birth city and Khartoum city, where the majority of his family lived.

After primary four, he moved to settle in Khartoum with the rest of his family. He was born to a family rich with educational values and family tradition values. His grandfather was an educational pioneer in the East Nile Provence as he established the first private primary school in Provence.

He was also a tribal chief and the mayor of all of his tribe's chiefs in Sudan.

So Badradeen grew up learning the wisdom and knowledge from his family and the doors of knowledge that they offered. However, He had left the country and settled in the UK back in 2011.

He holds a Highers in IT and a Highers in Social Sciences and is now pursuing a degree in Psychology

Foreword

By

Emily Bryson

I first met Badradeen when he attended my Intermediate ESOL (English for Speakers of Other Languages) class back in 2012. He had newly arrived in Scotland from Sudan.

All the students in the class were New Scots, who had left their previous lives in various parts of the world to settle in Glasgow. At the time, Badradeen must have been around eighteen, so he was one of the youngest in the class.

It was quickly obvious that Badradeen was one of those students that glued the class together. His smile was always welcoming and he'd be happy to help others with their work or navigating their new city.

What made him really stand out from the crowd was his writing. When he submitted written work, you could see he'd taken time to add idioms, advanced level adjectives and bring the piece to life with imagery and descriptions. It was always a pleasure to read.

As he moved up the levels of English, other teachers noticed this too. Jenifer Martin, another of his teachers, had a project where her class teamed up with an English Communications class. Together, they created various poems, short stories and other creative works. They then presented these at The Scotia bar in Glasgow.

Although I wasn't his teacher any more, Badradeen invited me along, and of course I accepted. I was so proud of him as he confidently shared his piece with the world. It seemed like he had been born for it.

Since then, we've stayed in touch. I feel honoured that he often shares his work with me and values my feedback. I'm no expert in poetry, but I know that I've enjoyed reading every one of his poems. I'm sure you will too.

Emily Bryson.

Badradeen Mohammad

An Ancient Story

A story

Revealing itself

An ancient story

Been saved in the shelf

A present story

Of all and oneself

A story

Revealing itself

Narrated in the past

Happened in the future

Of all and oneself

A story

Revealing itself

A Letter to My Unborn Child

O son, life will teach you a lot

Hurts you a lot

Makes you cry a lot

And will make you laugh a lot

Take advantage of its lessons

You will love it to the extent of insanity

And you might hate it sometimes

That's life, a combination of odds.

Enjoy its beauty as much as you can

And be patient about its bitterness, as you can

When it laughs with you, laugh with it and be grateful for its generosity.

And when it gives you a harsh face, do not complain

Be sure that no matter how long the night became

Dawn will come after all, and that nothing lasts forever

Live it with hope and optimism you will be happy

O child, do not prohibit yourself from happiness

Learn as much as you can

Play and be cheerful as much as you can

One day, you will grow

You will change a little

You will make mistakes

And you will see life from different angles

Choose your angle wisely

Before you sleep, review your day.

If you found that there is something which you could have done better

Do not hesitate to do it if you got the chance again

Better your choices you will sleep with clear, conscience

Respect others. You will be respected

And do good no matter how little it is

Do not hate anything, and love as much as you can

As love is the immanence of life

The Moonlight

It seems so easy

To climb the height

It looks so nice

When it's all bright

Never looked so dark.

Under the moonlight

Its light sprays

gives us a good sight

It needs courage

To continue the ride

But it seems so easy.

To climb the height

Endeavour is important

To win a fight

Badradeen Mohammad

Knowledge is a key

To gain insight

8

But it seems so easy.

Under the moonlight

The Nile River

The river Nile ran

Is been running ever since

Travelled through countries

Has lakes

Branches as well

Visited Tanzania

Congo

Uganda, where it rested well

Then moved to Sudan

Fed from Deer sea

Giraffes sea

Arabs sea

Dinder, Rahad

and continued its way

It is called the White Nile

Its other part started from Ethiopia.

Visited Sudan

Linked with Atbaras's river

Qash river

And other branches

Made the Blue Nile

Both merged in Khartoum.

Surrounded Totti Island

Then continued its journey to the north

Here, there, in the mergence

The birth of the mighty Nile announced

Ran through the desert

Irrigated farms and palm gardens

Created seven waterfalls

Along its way

Then reached Egypt

Irrigated Egyptian lands

Watered thirsty mouths

As it used to from its start

Lightened the countries visited

With Electricity

Then, finally rested in

The mediterranean sea

A remarkable journey

Made it the longest

River Nile

The Nile river

Badradeen Mohammad

I Met You, My Friend

I met you, my friend

Coincidentally

As we were both invited

to the same event

I didn't look at the crowd a lot

Quickly went outside

After my slot

There was a garden

Each table had two

benches beside

Then you joined me

Although we hadn't had

Physically met before

Only in metaphors

But we knew each other

I was sitting on a bench.

Although there was another

Bench linked to the table

You sat on the table

And rested your head

You consulted me on writing a poem

You said you have feelings there

might be war-breaking

I told you

Don't worry, my friend

People here won't get into war

But it's the nature of their talking

Then, a woman came out of the tent

Shouted

Do you know how many poems

You owe me Badradeen

I told her honestly not

But I will look them out

If you gave me your name

She wrote her blog name.

On my phone and went back.

You told me

Listen my friend

I really need to go

But my daughter

Is getting her face painted

Let me see if it is done

I said ok my friend

Then I woke up

I Am from Sudan

I am from the place where history had started

And civilisation had began

I am from the place where black pharaohs had once ruled and
conquered a huge part of the land.

In fact, most pharaohs were black

But there's something about history

You can't, and you won't understand

I am from the place where the white and blue Niles merged and
announced the birth of the mighty Nile in a soil full of sand.

I'm from the land of the blacks

That's the translation for my country's name

And if you still wonder,

I am from the Sudan

Badradeen Mohammad

Storms

Storms often destroy
But wise storms build
While moving against
The norm

Storms run so fast
Hurting the planet
Wise storm moves slowly
Making a difference

Storms often make dispersion.
Wise storm
Creates divergence
To bring us all together

There're storms, wise.
Also, there are wise storms.
They do exist

She is a Belter

Yeah

That's right

Her smile is genuine

Beats you

With no fight

Her eyes are charming

You'd fall for them

From the very

First sight

Yeah

She is a belter

Badradeen Mohammad

No Need to Explain

I'd rather ignore

What people said

And rest my brain

Survive

Is there a sea that I can drown in

And still, survive

Is there a fire I can walk through

And still alive

If I lost the way one day

Will I be on time arrive

Seas are seas in the end

Might swallow you

Even if you know how to dive

Dive if you got to dive

But you got to make sure you survive

Regulator

A navigator

Navigates time

A regulator

Regulates time

He always on

The move

The Dead Man

A dead man walking

A dead man talking

And throwing some nice stuff

The dead man flattering

The dead man flirting

Then became a flirt

And living some real stuff

The dead man loses

Because he supposed to be dead

And well prepared for some real stuff

He felt the longing to his teenage time

He used to believe in himself at that time

So he did some regular teenage stuff

Is the dead man still dead?

I doubt so!

He living some real life stuff.

Differences

Poorness is not the lack of money

It is the lack of ethics and morals.

Richness is not the richness of money

It is the richness of the self.

Differences we don't pay attention to,

but if we did,

we live with satisfaction and contentment.

For the quality of life, I speak.

Togetherness

There's nothing better.

Than togetherness

Badradeen Mohammad

Nothing to Hide

I've got nothing to hide;

nothing to show

I'm warm as the sun

cool as the snow

I like to joke, sing, dance

and sometimes draw

I ride the words;

up high and low

Fly with the vibes;

dive into the meanings,

deep and slow

Ruins of Memories

On a sunny autumn day

I was leaning on a plastic chair in front of the family house

With sweat dripping from my body

Caused by the high temperature

And resentment for the intensity of my anger

Suddenly, without realising I found myself standing up

So fascinated by the landscape

The breathtaking beauty and charm

This was magnificence and harmony, which I had not found in any instance of my life.

A cluster of white clouds and, in just moments, fantastic coloured

Were formed in red-dark, and others were black and grey

Added to the sky was like a page draped in Lothario blue

Like a masterful painting, fine

Drawn by a skilled artist

Which did not leave any room for error

Everyone was running down, looking for a shelter to escape the heavy rain

I did not move a finger

Amused by the romance that took me to mazes of straying and day-
dreams

And with each drop of water, I felt recovery

As it was cleansing me from dirty days

At the peak of my happiness

I relaxed to the rhythms of memories, which revived my soul

And made me see the world in its most beautiful

And in the most wonderful moments, I lived

Sitting on the ruins of memories

Suddenly, I found myself shouting and swearing at a driver

Who drove his car through the water in front of me

So that water splashed full of dirt and filth

Spread over my body and my clothes

Marking the end of the dream and those moments

Only then I realised

Life does not give us all we wish for

Even in our dreams

Unless it wanted to

An Apology to Love

I won't ask you why had you left

And I won't even judge

Perhaps I was the wrong

And stupidly said goodbye

I won't tell you how much I was hurt

Or how many nights I spent on crying

As I had been the worst and the devil

By being stupidly cool and shy

I'm sorry that I hurt you.

By misunderstanding your eyes

And the silent love on them

I'm sorry for the pain that I caused

At every time you waited me to show

I'm sorry for the move that I couldn't make

When your eyes had shown mine the signs of acceptance

And I'm sorry that I hurt the most girl I liked and respected

I'm sorry that I hurt you.

I'm sorry that I hurt me.

And love

28

Sounds Like

Sounds like there's no sound in the music

Feels like there's no feeling in the dance

But the audience are enjoying the show

So, should we dance to please the audience

Or should the crowd sing us a song

So we can feel the dance

Perhaps we should just join the audience

Happenings

We were all taught that

every happening has a reason

and we do all believe it

scientists said

every action has a reaction

we believe them, too

and yet,

happenings still happen

with unknown reasons

and reactions sometimes come

with no signs of actions!

Right Time

There's no right time.

Better than right now

Badradeen Mohammad

Silent Love

Oh, lady, don't be puzzled

I loved you in silence

And my love is the most dangerous secrets

My love is like fire if caught

it burns up all the trees

And my love is like a sea if flooded

It does not know the meaning of fences

Pieces

Collecting pieces

Pieces of myself

Reviewing memories

Memories from the past

Not the past of history

The past of mine

I used to be me

I shout in silence

Now, where have I lost

Is my job to find out

So I'm looking around

Turning around

Losing rounds

Winning rounds

Just collecting pieces

Badradeen Mohammad

The Girl of My Dreams

The girl of my dreams has made me cry

When she came right next to me

and said no, hi

The one that had made my heart dance and sing

Under the wonderful blue sky

Had said no, hi

Acted like she didn't see when she passed by

I know that move; I know that lie

The girl of my dreams had made me cry

Be Creative

Be creative when you write.

Be creative when you talk.

Be creative when you smile.

Be creative even at work.

Dreams

They come so often

Show us a glimpse of light.

Mind, heart, Heart, mind

Mind heart

Heart mind

Mind

Mind speaks

With no fear

Heart

Heart cries

With no tear

Mind

Mind is sharp

Like a spear

Heart

Heart is kind

It can bear

Mind

Mind is fast

With no gear

Heart

Heart is humble

Doesn't know fear

Only fear God

Badradeen Mohammad

The Heart

Life
Starts from Within
Within the heart
Happiness
Starts from Within
Within the heart
Love
Starts from Within
Within the heart
Dreams
Start from within
Within the heart
Strength
Starts from Within
Within the heart
It all comes
Down to the heart

I look for you

I look for you at all times
I look at poetry
In historic stories
And in melodies

I look for a home
that contains my soul
makes me carefree
Extinguishes the fire
of longing in my heart
and drives away grief
from my life

I look for you in the silence
of the night
your spectrum comes
like a dream
tickles my heart as children
and throw arrows
of love at me
then I fall with juvenile joy

The dream comes

as fast as lightning

stops the bloodstream

in my heart for seconds

and the spectrum

hovers over me

scatters roses and scents

then your fragrance

emits everywhere

O moon that if appeared

Lit up the place

O hope dwells my sentiment

if you would come, hurry

I long to meet you

waiting since birth

and my longings are

erupting like a volcano

Quiescence

No words to be read

No talk to be heard

No feelings to be felt

No situation to be explained

But deep quiescence

And a silent song to be played

Badradeen Mohammad

Friends

What a good friend you are

Kind-hearted

Pure soul

To me is a star

Friends

What a good friend you are

You know your value

You know where you are

Friends

What a good friend you are

The Inner Peace

In life, you will go through a lot

You will lose loved ones

You might experience fear

fear from the unknown

As in certain points

you will be close to despair

feel everything you worked for

is far from being achievable

Then you have to realise God

has chosen you to experience all these events

in order to teach you

To help you find you in this life

and if you found you

You will feel the inner peace

Life

Life is full of holes

we might stumble

we might fall

but we got to know ourselves

what we're capable of

and how to stand after all

It is Not Good for You

My friend

It is not good for you

Not for your nerve

Nor for your immune system

Neither for your mind

Nor your thinking

So, stand for yourself

And quit drinking

P.S

My friend

You know I love

If not, I wouldn't tell

I don't want to

see you sick

Or go to hell

Excuse me

My talk might be harsh

But for your sake

I thought

I must tell

45

Badradeen Mohammad

Words

Words

Are so hard to swallow

For the haters

Of freedom

Peace Ambassadors

Soon, peace, love and unity will be spread all over the world

there will be no town or city that isn't filled with love

And from there, the real good life starts, and we will thank the informal peace ambassadors.

Do Not Judge People

Do not judge people

by the way, they look

If you must judge

judge yourself

Do not speak about people

by what you don't know

As people have tongues

but pretend to be deaf

If you looked after yourself

it would be better for you and them

And build your life

maybe one day you'll reach the top

You might know people

but you don't know what within themselves

People are types in thinking and understanding

Unique

She is quite unique

In an usual way

She means everything

That she'd say

Coincidences are great

When they happen

God's way

I don't how to describe her

There're no words

I can say

But

She's over there

Full of fun

Seeds

The flowers

Have seeds

Trees

Have seeds

Thoughts

Have seeds

Change

Have seeds

And I'm in love

With the seeds

The Journey of My Life

A painful journey

With no end

A long story

With no details

A dry space

In the middle of the green

And a garden with plants

Grown dead

Was the journey of my life

When it first seemed

Seemed a perfect journey

With no perfection

With flashing lights

But lasting flashes

The hope had lost

But moved through

52

A dream had died

I carried it, too

Some dreams are aims.

Aims come true

The journey continued

No matter high or low

Some journeys are simply journeys.

Perhaps

Simple journeys are part of the show.

Dear Mother

Dear mother

Your teachings were valued.

Shaped the man I am

Your knowledge was wide.

Helped me to learn and understand

Your support was remarkable.

Kept the hope alive

Even when I left the land

Your kindness is unique.

You planted it in our sand.

P.s

The soil still remembers.

Badradeen Mohammad

The Sun

The Sun disappeared
Left the roses pale

The Sun disappeared
Feared the sky to tell

The Sun disappeared
But was excused

Knock Knock

Knock knock

Who's there?

A visitor

Visiting who?

Your heart

Do I know you?

You don't

But I do

I don't open my heart easy.

Cause it won't close.

When I do

But remember

If you knocked

Don't plan to go

Badradeen Mohammad

Love

Love isn't a game
It's not right to touch
Someone's heart
And leave them in vain

Love isn't a game
L
For loyalty
O
For obsession
V
For vividness
E
For equal chances of rain

Love isn't a game

I Asked for You

I asked for you

In the mornings

And at night

I asked for you

Under the Sun rays

And under the moonlight

You know I did

Badradeen Mohammad

If You Ask

If you ask

The sky is clear

So is the mind

The Naked Poem

I decided to get naked.

Seriously, I mean it.

I am tired of wearing a dress

That brings me down to hell

And causes me stress

So I decided to get naked

You remember when we first met.

You asked if I love

And I reacted like a fool and said

I don't know, love, then you got upset

You said I am cruel, cold and careless

Living alone by myself

with no feelings of loneliness

That was because I was wearing the dress of fear

As love is frightness

And an easy way to death

Unless it is a real love

Yes, I seemed quite strange.

I kept silent in the matter of talk

Smiled in the matter of sadness

You asked if I was in pain

Or my sorrows were burning me inside

I know you was trying to help

But I got mad and said

I feel no pain and no need for hugs

That was because I was wearing the dress of strength

That dress gave me enough stress

But I can not go without it

You hurt me once

I just reacted with a smile

You hurt me twice

My smile didn't change

That was just because I was wearing

The dress of respect and forgiveness

That dress is priceless

You remember when I hugged you?

It was an innocent hug.

And accidentally, I grabbed a kiss.

A cheek kiss

That was just because my desire wasn't wearing a dress.

Honestly, I don't leave it undressed.

Unless I lost to my weakness

Then, I dropped the dress of shyness

And told you how much I love you

But you just quit

You wanted to kill me with jealousy

And celebrate the fake victory

But I surprised you with happiness

That wasn't because I can't get rude

It was just because I was wearing

The dress of abstinence and politeness

I can easily take off.

But I won't do so

It is such an adorable dress.

You know what

I think it was your idea to get me naked

While I love to be dressed

So, I will keep all of my dresses

One day, you will come with regret and yet

I might wear the dress of forgiveness

And might I simply hug you with love

As love is powerful

And sometimes it refuses to be dressed

Strong

They tried to prove me wrong.

But I stood strong

Fighting their battles of wits

From sunset till dawn

Badradeen Mohammad

My Angel

I waited you for long

I longed for you for long

But you don't seem to feel my heart

You don't seem to hear my song

So it's time to recover.

It's time to move on.

It's time to look for me.

It's time to be strong.

My angel, I waited you for long

The sky had felt my pain

Had shed tears of rain

But you don't seem to be there

Left me in my love chains

My angel, I wish you joy.

I wish you laughter

And happiness everlasting

But me I've got to move on

I've got to be strong

The Ghost of My Past

Lookin up

Lookin down

Just tryin' to see

How things were gone

N' how they gonna be

Sorrows in my heart

Bite me like a bee

The ghost of my past

Still follows me

Standing among my sorrows

Tryin' hard to see

Where is my way

N' the man I used to be

Let It Go

I can't claim what is not mine

What is went, let it go

I can't repeat the past

So, for the future, I grow

Scaredy Fish

Who am I to tell you to write

Who am I to ask you to teach

Who am I to ask you to learn

And who am I to ask you to preach

Who am I to ask you to jog

And who am I to ask you to fish

Who am I to ask you to shout

And who am I to ask you to reach

Who am I to ask you to fight

And who am I to ask you to resist

Who am I to ask you to govern right

And who am I to tell you about this

I am just a scaredy fish

Badradeen Mohammad

Lonesome

In my lonesome

I did nothing

Read nothing

In my lonesome

I cried nothing

Looked for nothing

In my lonesome

I got bored sometimes

But smiled often

In my lonesome

I saw you here

And I said nothing

In my lonesome

I dived deep

But it seemed for nothing

The Mountains

Rocks can be taken every day

from a mountain

Rocks can be broken every day

on a mountain

But the mountain remains always

a mountain

Badradeen Mohammad

Don't Bother

Buddy, don't bother

if life became so dark

try to be the light

if pain reached your heart

keep tears away inside

smile to the world

who knows if you cry alone at night

people can see your wounds

not the sorrows you hide

Remember

Pain sea can be wide

Joy space is sometimes tight

Buddy, don't bother

tomorrow is just a dream

and yesterday had gone

just focus on what you aim

and if someone told you you are a fool

don't bother,

things are not always as they seem

Badradeen Mohammad

Arguments

A step forward, then another back

a repeated action that I used to do since the day I met myself

we haven't been always on the same spot; perhaps we have had

haven't been always on the right way

as I've lost balance in cases of rush and teenage rage

and haven't been always with sometimes, I enjoy being against

when I usually follow my own

there are always arguments between myself and I

sometimes, myself starts the row, and sometimes, I

whenever my heart makes a decision, my mind unjustly turns the
table upside down

and moves me from a joy a state to cry

and yet, my heart naturally forgets

not even with a sign of regret

while others usually get upset

but I won't get more than my fate, so

when I am down, I don't look so down

and when I am up, I am just in the middle of the line

I leave emotions to fight against emotions, sometimes the weak
emotions die

and sometimes, some emotions win the rest

honestly, I don't care which of them are the best

as long as they all come from the bottom

the same thing for feelings as when they fight against each other

I used to stupidly react with a smile

and forget the fact that a smile isn't always enough

nor the right thing to react with

but I say to myself, why should you stay in pain

while you can simply smile and breathe

I've tried to run away from myself, but wisdom has never let me do
so

it used to grab me from my confusion and put me on track

then create beginnings after each end

you know, last night, I thought I wrote a love poem

but I woke up this morning with a political poem

Badradeen Mohammad

I don't know what brought politics into love

I mean, it all sounds complete madness

in fact, I am not even interested in politics

but as wise people say, different seeds seem always different

but they give us the same shadow despite

and today is not far from yesterday nor the day before

they all have the same shape, and yet we who play the rest

and to be the best, in my point of view, does not mean to be better
than others

whilst it means to be the best at who you are

so I always try to do the best I can to achieve the best of me

Shots

Shot in the leg
Continued playin'

Shot in the chest
Rib broken
But stood the same

Shot in the heart
Just stitched it
And kept sane

Shot in the head
That was too much
So quit the game

Badradeen Mohammad

When It Comes To Love

When it comes to love

My mind says

Don't do it

It is too high

If you fall

You might die

Then my heart says

Don't worry

Give it a try

If you survived

You might fly

Your Eyes

When the eyes look at the eyes

It's always a normal look

But when yours look at mine

It's definitely something else

I feel like there's no one in the room

Except you, your eyes, and me looking at them

My blood pressure goes up

And suddenly down

With no signs of balance

I feel my body going outside the scope of gravity

And realise all what Franklin had said about similarities is true

And your eyes prove Newton wrong

As I fall up in front of them

Not down as that poor apple did

Then I forgot about her and them

About me or him

About where and when

All I see is just you and your adorable eyes

I see scattered messages all over the space of your eyes

I try to collect them

Open them

Read them

Or even translate them into love signs

I always seem to draw blank

I travel through your eyes to the mazes of charm

Trying to manipulate the reality

But whenever I feel I almost got there

Just something or someone interrupts our silence

And a pale smile will be drawn on my face

They are quite bossy.

And like twisters, your eyes

I mean, I used to read girls eyes

And I used to be a damn romantic

But time has played roughly

So I can't distinguish your romance

From yours being nice

I admit the fact that I love them

And figured out my level of understanding

Still hasn't reached the level of your eyes speech

So I got high tonight

I thought, might I, could I be able to read messages that your eyes
had sent from that point of highness.

But I come from my journey with nothing

But confusion

Every time I try to run away from your eyes

I eventually bump into them

Even tonight, when I decided not to think of them

I accidentally wrote this poem

Badradeen Mohammad

Windows

The heart beating

Beating rapidly

Then it calms down

Just like playin' a rhythm

From deep within

Where memories

Had been locked

We open a window

And look

Look back through it

Try to fix

What needs to be fixed

Stitches

It's the heart that needs stitches

It's the heart that needs to heal

it's the soul that wants to fly

it's the soul that needs to feel

Badradeen Mohammad

My Words

I told you I joke

O God

I miss that part

I sing on my own

I don't think that's hard

Finally

Still got the moves tho

And my words

From the heart

I Need You

I need you

Yeah, I really do

But I can't say it now

I can't tell you so

Time has changed me

Maybe it did that to you

I'm still flying solo

But you now got a boo

We were a perfect match

But I wasn't ready, tho

You went so far alone

And I love that in you

I won't pull you back

It's a selfish thing to do

Can't claim the love

After all, I put you through

We destined to love each other

In our own points of view

I better say nothing

I better let you go

My timing is always wrong

Badradeen Mohammad

My love is overdue

So I can't reveal it now

I can't tell so

My Friend

Her eyes are green
Her heart is white

I couldn't see its color.
But I can see its light.

Her face is so pretty.
So is her name

I met her in Patras
I met her at the train.

I was so unsettled
I was so in vain

She helped to focus
She became my friend.

Badradeen Mohammad

In Love

A man who he afraid to love

A man who he in love again

A man who he afraid to lose

The precious diamond he ever seen

A man who he enjoys the sun

A man who he feels the rain

Your Parents

Look after your parents.

As long as they're alive

Look after your siblings

Your relatives

Your neighbours

Your friends

And your wife

It's a sort of worship

Pure Soul

I drunk

It didn't do me good

So I said no to drinks

I smoked

It didn't do me good

So I said no to drugs

Clear mind

Pure soul

Aah My Pen

I lost looking for a pen.

Which lost during the fun

Under the moonlight

I used to describe with it.

The moon face

At the beautiful nights

It was inspiring and

Formulates words like pearls

Some of them are

Meaningful

Some are wisdoms

Some are lessons

In the silence of the night

I looked without boredom

In the dread of its darkness

The hope wasn't lost

Badradeen Mohammad

I looked with eyes

And hands

With no tiredness

In the fearful dreariness

Of the night

I cried

And to that shiny pale moon

I complained

Friends came and went.

No one knew

What I talked about

I asked him

Where is the pen

Said

Why are you crying

I answered

You think it will be

Easy for me

To separate

From my family

And he is one of them

Will it be easy for me?

To part

From my friend

And companion

All this cries for a pen.

Said

A valuable pen

I said

I found it

He answered

Aah my pen

I longed for long

Been distanced

For long

Been abandoned

For long

Been travelling

For long

Father

Father

I miss you, my friend

I still remember

Our laughs

Banters

And the things we said

I wished to see you

One last time

But I have to accept the fate

O father

I miss you, my friend.

Badradeen Mohammad

The Tiger in the Woods

He was first a tiger.

A tiger in the wood

A dragon in the sky

And a knight in the hood

He was first a tiger.

A tiger in the wood

Gardens

Garden of palms
Give us dates

Seeds of good deeds
Grant us gardens in heaven.

Gardens of flowers
Make our days brighter.

Brighter days
Give us hope

Brighter future
isn't just movies

Wisdom and knowledge
are the key

Gardens of truth
Give us plain fruits
But fresh

A smile

A smile can say a lot.

Just a smile

Genuine smile

With soft banter

Can make the day brighter

A smile can do a lot.

When it meant to say

What's the tongue

Can't talk

A smile

Just a smile

Can say a lot

From Couch to Marathon: A Beginner's Guide to Running 26.2 miles

Table of Contents